Meals of Many Lands

A COOKBOOK FOR CHILDREN

Recipes Compiled by Miriam B. Loo

This book is dedicated to all children who are discovering the joys of cooking, and especially to my own grandchildren, Susan, James, Anne, Julia and Tara.

Designed by Marsha Winborn

Kitchen Safety Rules

1. Keep the handles of any pots and pans on the stove turned inward so you can't knock them and spill something or burn yourself.

2. Always use a dry pot holder or oven mitt when handling pots and pans. Wet pot holders won't keep out heat.

3. Water will not splash if you put foods gently into boiling water. Lift lids from hot pots with the opening away from you.

4. Dish towels, pot holders and recipes should not be left too near a hot burner — they can catch on fire. So can loose clothes, long sleeves and long hair, so be sure to tie your hair back and roll up your sleeves.

5. **Do not** put hot grease into water, or water into hot grease. In case of a grease fire, turn off the oven or burner, stand back, and toss handfuls of baking soda at the base of the flame. Call for help.

6. When you're finished cooking, always make sure all oven and stove dials are turned OFF.

7. Keep wet hands away from electrical outlets.

8. Always pick up a knife by its handle, not its blade. When cutting, always cut away from yourself.

Helpful Hints

1. Make a list of the foods you will need and help with the shopping — it's fun!

2. Always check with an adult before you use the kitchen.

3. Wash your hands before handling food.

4. Gather everything you need before you start. You may find it helpful to set the table ahead of time, too.

5. Put on a good, big apron to cover you up.

6. For best results, always follow the recipe exactly at first. After a while, you can try variations.

7. Use a timer to tell you when the cooking time is up.

8. Do things quietly and don't get excited.

9. Clean up when you are finished and put everything away.

How to Set a Table

SALAD PLATE

GLASS

DINNER PLATE

CUP AND SAUCER

DINNER FORK

SALAD FORK

KNIFE

SPOON

NAPKIN

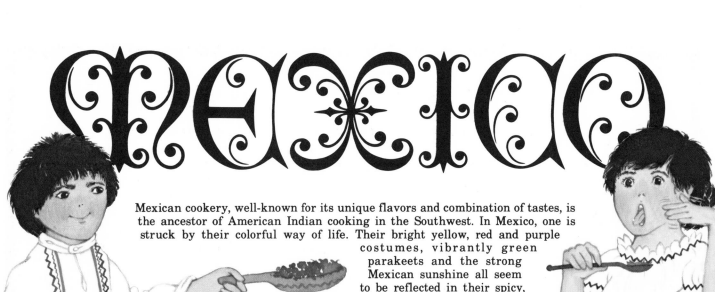

MEXICO

Mexican cookery, well-known for its unique flavors and combination of tastes, is the ancestor of American Indian cooking in the Southwest. In Mexico, one is struck by their colorful way of life. Their bright yellow, red and purple costumes, vibrantly green parakeets and the strong Mexican sunshine all seem to be reflected in their spicy, tasty food.

Because Mexicans enjoy a mild climate and generally fertile soil, they have many fruits and vegetables to use in their dishes. Maize, a type of corn, is the mainstay, with squash, tomatoes, beans, onions and many tropical fruits to add flavor. Cheese made from goat's milk is also important in the diet. The bread of Mexico is the "tortilla," made from corn. "Frijoles" (beans of various kinds), are as old a food as maize and furnish an inexpensive protein. Mexicans enjoy drinking cocoa, coffee and other "refrescoes" of fruit juices sweetened with fresh honey and brown sugar. Hot herb drinks such as camomile, oregano and sage tea are also served with meals.

Your Mexican Supper Menu
for 6 People at 7 P.M.

GUACAMOLE SALAD
NACHOS · TACOS
LIME SHERBET WITH STRAWBERRIES
MEXICAN COCOA

Defrost Guacamole

Prepare Guacamole

GUACAMOLE SALAD

HAVE READY	YOU'LL NEED
2 cans frozen guacamole, defrosted	can opener
	medium mixing bowl
1 large tomato, chopped	mixing spoon
2 tablespoons bacon bits	paring knife
½ teaspoon Tabasco® sauce	chopping board
6 lettuce leaves, washed and drained on paper towel	measuring spoons
	paper towel
tortilla chips	serving platter

Spoon defrosted guacamole into mixing bowl. Add chopped tomato, bacon bits and Tabasco® sauce. Mix well. Cover and refrigerate. To serve, arrange 6 lettuce leaves on serving platter. Spoon 6 equal amounts of guacamole onto lettuce leaves. Decorate with 6 tortilla chips stuck in each serving. At the table, pass the platter and let your guests help themselves.

JUST BETWEEN US: Guacamole can be a delicious dip to serve before dinner or for a snack. Just serve with chips or raw vegetables such as carrot sticks, celery sticks or cherry tomatoes.

4

TACOS
(Makes 12 tacos)

HAVE READY	YOU'LL NEED
2 pounds lean ground beef	large skillet with lid
2 packages taco seasoning	large mixing spoon
1 box taco shells	cookie sheet
½ head lettuce, shredded	paring knife
½ pound grated Cheddar cheese	chopping board
	cheese grater
1 medium onion, chopped	can opener
2 medium tomatoes, chopped	5 bowls
	2 pot holders
1 8-ounce can taco sauce	serving platter

MEAT SAUCE: Brown meat in skillet over medium-high heat. Spoon off excess grease. Add 2 packages of taco seasoning and cook according to directions on package. Turn off heat and cover meat sauce until 10 minutes before serving. Reheat on low for 10 minutes. Fill warmed taco shells with meat sauce. Serve on platter.

TACO SHELLS: 10 minutes before serving, just as you begin to reheat the sauce, put shells on cookie sheet and heat in oven at 200° for 10 minutes.

TOPPINGS: Put lettuce, grated cheese, onions, tomatoes and taco sauce in separate bowls on the table. Let your guests select their own toppings.

"Onion's skin very thin,
Mild winter coming in.
Onion's skin thick and tough,
Coming winter cold and rough."

(Prepare early afternoon)

NACHOS
(To be served as an appetizer. Makes 24 Nachos.)

YOU'LL NEED	HAVE READY
cookie sheet	1 5-ounce vacuum-packed can round tortilla chips
cheese grater	
measuring spoons	¼ pound Cheddar cheese, grated
can opener	
2 pot holders	1 4-ounce can taco sauce
serving platter	

Fill cookie sheet with 24 tortilla chips. Top each chip with 1 heaping teaspoon of cheese and ¼ teaspoon taco sauce. 15 minutes before serving time, preheat oven to 350°. Place in oven for 5 minutes or until cheese is melted. Serve right away on serving platter.

LIME SHERBET WITH STRAWBERRIES

(Remove strawberries from freezer at 5:00.)

HAVE READY
1 quart lime sherbet
1 1-pound package
  frozen sweetened
  strawberries

YOU'LL NEED
spoon
6 small bowls

Spoon sherbet into bowls and top with strawberries. Serve with Mexican Cocoa.

(Begin preparation at 4:30)

MEXICAN COCOA

HAVE READY
4 cups milk
1 4-ounce milk chocolate
  candy bar
1 teaspoon ground
  cinnamon
1 teaspoon vanilla

YOU'LL NEED
small saucepan
measuring cups
wooden spoon
measuring spoons
wire whisk
6 cups

OLD BELIEF:
If you find bubbles on your milk or coffee, drink them up before they disappear and you will be rich.

Pour milk into saucepan. Add the chocolate and stir over medium heat until chocolate is melted. Remove from heat and add the cinnamon and vanilla. Set aside. At serving time, return to heat and beat the mixture with a whisk until it is frothy and hot. Pour into cups. Serve with the lime sherbet.

6

CHINA

Chinese recipes are well-kept family secrets passed down from generation to generation. In the words of an ancient Chinese saying: "A well-prepared dish should appeal to the eye by its coloring, to the nose by its aroma, to the ear by its sound (such as crunch, crunch) and, of course, to the mouth by its flavor." A complete Chinese meal is carefully planned to provide a contrast of textures and colors as well as a variety of flavors.

It is surprising in a country as vast as China that there are few differences in the dishes from one region to another. The four basic Chinese foods are rice, soybeans, pork and chicken. Vegetables vary in availability from district to district. The Chinese are economical cooks, nothing is ever wasted, and from basic ingredients these people have created an enormous range of delicious dishes.

Chinese children, like the Japanese, learn to handle delicate chopsticks at an early age. In contrast to the Japanese tradition of eating at a low table while seated on the floor, the Chinese dine at a table with chairs. The young respectfully wait for their elders to be seated, and for a nod of assent before taking their places.

Your Chinese Buffet Menu
for 6 People at 7 P.M.

EGG DROP SOUP · CHINESE SALAD
SWEET & SOUR PORK · RICE
ICE CREAM WITH MANDARIN
ORANGES & FORTUNE COOKIES
SERVE WITH HOT TEA

CHINESE SALAD

HAVE READY		**YOU'LL NEED**	
2 large cucumbers	2 teaspoons sugar	vegetable peeler	measuring cups
2 green or red bell peppers, washed	1 teaspoon salt	paring knife	measuring spoons
8 to 10 radishes, washed	¼ teaspoon pepper	chopping board	mixing spoon
2 celery ribs, washed	2 tablespoons soy sauce	medium bowl	small skillet
⅔ cup vegetable oil	2 teaspoons toasted	small bowl	serving bowl
4 tablespoons cider vinegar	sesame seeds		

Peel the cucumbers and slice into thin rounds. Cut into quarters and remove the seeds from the peppers and then slice each quarter lengthwise into thin slices. Slice the radishes and celery into thin slices. Put all the vegetables into a medium bowl. In a small bowl mix the vegetable oil, vinegar, sugar, salt, pepper and soy sauce. Pour over the vegetables. Carefully mix the vegetables and dressing, turning so as not to mash the vegetables. Cover and put in refrigerator to chill. Mix again before serving and sprinkle with sesame seeds. (To toast sesame seeds, place in dry skillet over medium heat and stir until golden. Be sure not to burn.)

RICE

HAVE READY	YOU'LL NEED	
¾ cup long-grain white rice	2-quart ovenproof dish with lid	mixing spoon 2 pot holders
2 cups boiling water	measuring cups	serving bowl
1 teaspoon salt	measuring spoons	

Put the rice in a 2-quart ovenproof dish. Add 2 cups boiling water and salt. Stir. Cover dish with lid or tightly with foil. Put in a 350° oven and bake for 45 minutes. Remove and check to be sure grains of rice are soft. When guests are ready to eat, serve with Sweet and Sour Pork.

OLD BELIEF:
A hungry person
will call if you
drop a dishrag.

SWEET & SOUR PORK

HAVE READY

		YOU'LL NEED	
1 tablespoon vegetable oil	1 medium green pepper	large skillet with lid	can opener
1½ pounds lean pork shoulder, cut in 2-inch by ½-inch strips	¼ cup firmly packed brown sugar	measuring spoons	3 small bowls measuring
½ cup water	2 tablespoons cornstarch	paring knife	cups
1 1-pound can pineapple chunks and syrup	¼ cup cider vinegar	chopping board	serving
	1 tablespoon soy sauce	mixing spoon	bowl
	½ teaspoon salt		

Put 1 tablespoon vegetable oil into skillet over medium heat. Add cut-up pork and brown. Then add ½ cup water, cover and simmer for 45 minutes over very low heat. While the meat is simmering, drain the pineapple. Save the syrup and set aside in bowl. Quarter and seed the green pepper, and cut lengthwise into strips. Set the pineapple and pepper aside. In a small bowl, combine the brown sugar and cornstarch; add the pineapple syrup, vinegar, soy sauce and salt. Mix well and add to the pork. Cook and stir until the sauce thickens and gets shiny. Add the pineapple and pepper and cook for 2 or 3 minutes more. Remove from heat and put in serving bowl. Serve with hot fluffy rice and pass extra soy sauce.

8

EGG DROP SOUP

HAVE READY

10 leaves spinach, washed and dried on a paper towel
4 large mushrooms, washed and dried on a paper towel and thinly sliced
1 egg, beaten
2 10½-ounce cans chicken broth
2 cans water
1 teaspoon soy sauce

YOU'LL NEED

paper towels
paring knife
egg beater and bowl
medium saucepan
can opener
mixing spoon
measuring spoons
soup ladle
6 soup bowls
6 soup spoons

Before you start the soup, be sure to have the spinach leaves washed and dried, the mushrooms washed, dried and thinly sliced, and the egg beaten. **Now,** pour the chicken broth and water into the saucepan. Heat over high heat until the mixture boils. Turn the heat down to medium and add the soy sauce. Next, carefully dribble the beaten egg into the **very** hot soup, stirring all the time. Drop the spinach leaves and sliced mushrooms into the soup. To serve, spoon hot soup into bowls.

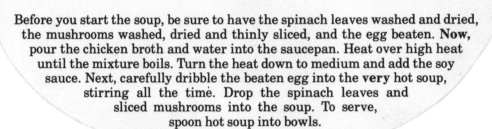

In marble halls as white as milk,
Lined with a skin as soft as silk,
Within a fountain crystal clear,
A golden apple doth appear.
No doors there are to this stronghold,
Yet thieves break in and steal the gold.

AN EGG

ICE CREAM WITH MANDARIN ORANGES & FORTUNE COOKIES

HAVE READY

1 quart vanilla ice cream
1 11-ounce can mandarin oranges
1 package fortune cookies

YOU'LL NEED

ice cream scoop
6 dessert bowls
can opener
plate for cookies

Place a scoop of ice cream in each bowl. Spoon oranges over each serving. Put cookies on plate to pass to guests.

Thirty-two white horses
On a red hill.
Now they stamp,
Now they champ,
Now they stand still.

TEETH

you have a secret admirer

ITALY

Italy was the first of all the European countries to develop a complete cooking style, and is recognized as the mother of European cuisine. Despite the tales of the gluttonous feasts of the Roman emperors, most of the dishes were created by the peasants. It was the farmers, shepherds and fishermen who developed the natural tastes of vegetables, meat and seafood.

Italian dishes vary greatly from region to region. This is partly because of the availability of olive oil in the south and butter in the north; and also because a hundred years ago the land consisted of many small city-states, each independent of the next. The people all developed individual styles of cooking, and this is still evident in their food.

Good things have a way of spreading, however. Pasta, originally from the south, is today eaten everywhere. There are said to be about 400 different kinds of pasta, from the wispy "capelli d'angelo" (angel's hair) to the giant "cannelloni" (large pipes), and including, of course, spaghetti and macaroni, long-time favorites of the American people.

Your Italian Pasta Party Menu
for 6 People at 7 P.M.

GREEN SALAD
WITH ITALIAN DRESSING
GARLIC BREAD · SPAGHETTI CASSEROLE
COFFEE TORTONI
RED WINE FOR ADULTS & MILK FOR CHILDREN

SPAGHETTI

LUMACHE

FUSILLI

CONCHIGLIE

CONCHIG-
LIETTE

EGG NOODLES

LASAGNE

RUOTE

BOWTIES

GROSSO RIGATO

ELBOW
MACARONI

RIGATONI

RAVIOLI

SPAGHETTI CASSEROLE

HAVE READY
2 tablespoons vegetable oil
1 pound lean ground beef
1 package spaghetti seasoning
2 15½-ounce cans of spaghetti in tomato sauce
½ cup canned grated Parmesan cheese

YOU'LL NEED
large skillet
measuring spoons
mixing spoon
can opener   2 pot holders
2-quart casserole   6 dinner plates
measuring cups

Place vegetable oil in skillet and heat over medium-high heat. Add meat and brown. Add the package of spaghetti seasoning. Stir well. Add the cans of spaghetti. Stir well. Pour the mixture into the casserole. Sprinkle the Parmesan cheese over the top. Bake in the oven at 350° for 30 minutes. (If you want, you can prepare the spaghetti early in the day and keep it in the refrigerator. Then heat it for 45 minutes at 350°. If using a glass casserole, let it stand at room temperature for one hour before putting it into a preheated oven.)

GREEN SALAD WITH ITALIAN DRESSING

HAVE READY
1 head of lettuce, washed, drained and dried with a paper towel
1 cucumber
⅓ cup Italian dressing

YOU'LL NEED
paper towel
salad bowl
vegetable peeler
paring knife
measuring cups
salad tossers

Tear the head of lettuce into bite-size pieces with your fingers. Peel and slice the cucumber. Add the cucumber slices to the lettuce in the salad bowl. Add ⅓ cup salad dressing and toss gently until all the lettuce and cucumbers have dressing on them.

JUST BETWEEN US: Add some of your own ideas — maybe chopped onion, bacon bits or chopped celery.

(Prepare day before or early morning)

COFFEE TORTONI

HAVE READY

¼ cup toasted almonds, finely chopped
1 egg white
1 tablespoon instant coffee
⅛ teaspoon salt
2 tablespoons sugar
1 cup whipping cream
¼ cup sugar
1 teaspoon vanilla
⅛ teaspoon almond extract

YOU'LL NEED

pie pan
2 mixing bowls
measuring spoons
mixing spoon
electric mixer
measuring cups
paring knife
chopping board
6 2-ounce paper cups

Place almonds in pie pan and put in preheated 325° oven to toast lightly. Remove and set aside. Combine egg white with coffee and salt in a mixing bowl. Beat it with your mixer until it forms soft peaks (see glossary) when you lift the mixer up. Slowly add the 2 tablespoons sugar and beat with mixer until stiff peaks (see glossary) form. Wash and dry the beaters and then whip the cream in the other mixing bowl until it forms soft peaks. (If mixing bowl, cream and beaters are chilled, this will help keep the cream from turning to butter when you whip it, especially in warm weather.) Next fold (see glossary) the ¼ cup sugar, vanilla and almond extract into the whipped cream. Then fold the almonds into the whipped cream. Now fold the whipped cream mixture into the egg white mixture. Spoon into the 6 paper cups and place in the freezer. Remove the desserts from the freezer before you sit down for dinner so that they can thaw a little bit.

GARLIC BREAD

HAVE READY

1 loaf French or Italian bread
1 stick butter or margarine, softened
garlic salt

YOU'LL NEED

bread knife
aluminum foil
2 pot holders

OLD BELIEF:
If you take the last piece of bread on a plate, you will be an old maid unless you kiss the cook.

Carefully slice the bread in 1-inch-thick slices. Spread a lot of butter or margarine on each slice. Sprinkle just a little bit of garlic salt on each slice. Wrap slices in foil like a loaf. At 6:30, place it in a 350° oven and bake for 30 minutes.

FRANCE

Because the French provinces vary greatly in their climate and geography, the type of food prepared also differs from region to region. One common element througout the country, however, is that just about all of the French people are deeply interested in good cooking and take a great deal of care over even the simplest everyday food. French boys and girls are introduced to cooking at an early age, and are encouraged to learn why things taste the way they do.

French Toast, called Pain Perdu (Pan Pare-dó), is said to have been the invention of a kindly French cook. Supposedly, a little boy and his sister had misbehaved so badly their father said they were to eat nothing but bread until they had mended their ways. The old cook who brought them their daily bread took sympathy upon them and prepared French Toast, which they ate delightedly. It is not known if they improved their behavior, but most likely, in time, they did.

Your French Breakfast Menu
for 4 People at 8 A.M.

FRESH FRUIT AND CREAM
FRENCH TOAST
CAFÉ AU LAIT

HAVE READY
1 pint of strawberries
or
4 bananas
½ cup powdered sugar
1 pint of
half-and-half cream

YOU'LL NEED
small knife   mixing bowl
mixing spoon   measuring cups
4 small serving bowls
cream pitcher

FRESH FRUIT AND CREAM

If using strawberries wash, drain and remove the green stems. Slice each berry in half and put in mixing bowl. If using bananas, peel and slice into mixing bowl. Add ½ cup of powdered sugar over berries or bananas and mix well. Spoon into individual bowls. Pour cream into a cream pitcher and place it on the table so your guests can pour cream over their fruit.

CAFÉ AU LAIT

HAVE READY
2 cups water
2 cups milk
6 teaspoons sugar
6 teaspoons instant coffee

YOU'LL NEED
measuring cups
saucepan
measuring spoons
small bowl
wire whisk
4 cups

Put the milk and water in a saucepan and bring to just boiling. Remove from heat. Mix the sugar and instant coffee together in a small bowl. Add four tablespoons of the hot milk and water to the coffee mixture, and stir together. Add the coffee mixture to the hot milk and water in the saucepan. Beat the mixture with a wire whisk until frothy and well mixed. Return the saucepan to the heat and bring to just boiling. Watch carefully so it does not over-run the pan. Remove from heat and serve.

FRENCH TOAST

HAVE READY
6 slightly beaten eggs
1 cup milk
½ teaspoon salt
1 tablespoon sugar
oil for frying
8 slices thick-cut bread,
  2 to 3 days old
maple-flavored syrup, powdered
  sugar or tart jelly

YOU'LL NEED
measuring cups
measuring spoons
mixing bowl
wire whisk
skillet
spatula
ovenproof plate
serving platter

In a shallow bowl, beat together the eggs, milk, salt and sugar with a wire whisk. Place the oil, about one tablespoon, in the skillet and heat over medium heat. (You may have to add more oil as you go along.) Dip the bread into the milk and egg mixture one slice at a time. Place each dipped slice into the hot oil in the frying pan. Do not overlap or crowd the pieces. Fry for 2 or 3 minutes (until golden brown) and then turn the slices over with the spatula and continue frying until the second side is golden brown. Put the browned slices on an ovenproof plate and place in a 200° oven to keep hot. Continue dipping and frying the remaining slices of bread. Serve hot with maple-flavored syrup, powdered sugar or tart jelly.

OLD BELIEF:
If you drop a
slice of bread with
the buttered side up,
a visitor will call.

RUSSIA

The proverb, "a man is made by the food he eats," is widely accepted in Russia. Here, flavorful, down-to-earth dishes have been created for centuries.

The U.S.S.R., covering ⅙ of the land of the world, has benefited from an abundance of foods. From their rye crops they make thick, black bread. Buckwheat groats have been used to make "kasha," a staple porridge, for centuries. Wild nuts, honey, berries, mushrooms, beef, pork and lamb abound. From the seas come sturgeon, salmon, eel, herring, trout, carp and pike. Stuffed vegetables are a favorite dish in southern regions, where groats have given way to rice. Sour cream is a national passion, a taste learned from the Tartars. Beef Stroganoff, the Russian meat dish most well-known abroad, was named for a gourmet and "bon vivant" (one who loves life) of the czarist court, Count Paul Stroganoff.

Russia is a land of exciting contrasts. It is a gigantic jigsaw puzzle of differing climates, landscapes, soils, peoples, customs and foods. Cooking styles differ somewhat throughout the fifteen republics, but it is the Slavic influence that predominates. The basic cuisine that has developed since the Slavs settled the land in the tenth century can be described as wholesome, hearty and plentiful, suitable for a cold climate and a hard-working people who practice the art of good cooking with unusual skill.

Your Russian Dinner Menu
for 4 People at 6:30 P.M.

GROUND BEEF STROGANOFF
RICE · TOMATOES & SOUR CREAM SALAD
MOCHA CHARLOTTE RUSSE · MILK

(Prepare the day before)

MOCHA CHARLOTTE RUSSE

HAVE READY

½ cup slivered almonds, toasted
½ teaspoon almond extract
1 1-pound bag marshmallows
½ cup milk
2 tablespoons instant powdered coffee
4 tablespoons unsweetened cocoa
1 cup whipping cream
2 tablespoons powdered sugar
2 packages ladyfingers

YOU'LL NEED

pie pan
double boiler (see glossary)
measuring spoons
measuring cups
wooden spoon
small mixing bowl
electric mixer
rubber bowl scraper
large mixing bowl
springform pan (see glossary)
cake plate

Place almonds in pie pan and put in preheated 325° oven until lightly browned. Watch carefully. Remove and set aside. Fill the lower pan of the double boiler half full with water and place the upper pan on top. Combine almond extract, marshmallows, milk, instant coffee and cocoa in the top of the double boiler. Place over medium-low heat. Stir until the marshmallows are melted. Remove from heat and let cool. In a small bowl, whip the cream with electric mixer until it forms soft peaks (see glossary). Add powdered sugar and whip until stiff peaks (see glossary) form. Fold whipped cream into the cooled marshmallow mixture with rubber bowl scraper. Line the sides and the bottom of the springform pan with the ladyfinger halves so that the cut sides are facing inward. Pour the marshmallow mixture into the lined pan. Sprinkle the top of the Mocha Charlotte Russe with the almonds. Put the springform pan into the freezer. Remove about 15 minutes before serving. Release the springform and place the dessert on a cake plate.

TOMATOES & SOUR CREAM SALAD

YOU'LL NEED
paring knife   mixing spoon
vegetable peeler   chopping board
medium bowl   measuring cups
measuring spoons   paper towels
4 salad plates

HAVE READY
4 small tomatoes
1 large cucumber
1 bunch of green onions
¼ cup dairy sour cream
¼ cup mayonnaise
¼ teaspoon salt
⅛ teaspoon pepper
lettuce leaves, washed
    and dried on paper
    towels

Wash tomatoes. Cut a slice off the top of the tomatoes about one inch down from the top. Scoop out the seeds. Place tomato shells upside down to drain and set aside. Peel and chop the cucumber into small pieces. Wash green onions and chop only the white parts of the onions into small pieces. Place onion and cucumber into medium bowl. Mix the sour cream, mayonnaise, salt and pepper, then fold into the cucumber mixture. Spoon into the tomato shells. Cover and refrigerate until you are ready to serve dinner. Place each tomato on a lettuce leaf which you have put on a salad plate.

I have eyes but cannot see;
A skin but not a face;
When farmers dig up ground for me
They find my hiding place.

A POTATO

RICE

To prepare rice, follow instructions for rice recipe in Chinese Menu, page 8.

GROUND BEEF STROGANOFF

YOU'LL NEED
large skillet
measuring spoons
paring knife
chopping board
measuring cups
wooden spoon
can opener
2-quart casserole
    dish

HAVE READY
2 tablespoons vegetable oil
⅓ cup chopped onion
⅛ teaspoon garlic powder
1 pound lean ground beef
2 tablespoons all-purpose
    flour
1 teaspoon salt
½ teaspoon paprika
1 10½-ounce can cream of
    chicken soup, undiluted
1 4-ounce can mushrooms,
    pieces and stems
1 cup plain yogurt or
    dairy sour cream
¼ cup chopped fresh parsley

Heat the vegetable oil in the skillet and add the onion. Sauté for 4 minutes, stirring, until onion is soft but not brown. Add the garlic powder and ground beef. Stir and cook the meat for about 10 minutes, until it is lightly browned. Add the flour, salt and paprika, mixing in well. Add the chicken soup and simmer for 10 minutes. Add the mushrooms and simmer another 10 minutes. Stir the yogurt or sour cream into the beef mixture and heat until very hot. Pour Beef Stroganoff over rice. Sprinkle the parsley over the top and serve.

SCANDINAVIA

There is a saying in Scandinavia that the Norwegians eat to live, the Swedes live to drink and the Danes live to eat. Unquestionably, the people of these Northern lands all dine very well.

Scandinavia is a name used to describe the northwestern European countries — including Denmark, Norway, Sweden, Iceland, Finland and the Faeroe Islands. The food of these fishing and shipping nations (where the Vikings lived 1,000 years ago) is pure and simple and very good. The main foods produced in this beautiful land are fish, home-grown vegetables and berries. Prepared dishes are rich with fine heavy cream and butter. Anyone travelling there is bound to come home a few pounds heavier, and the following meal is sure to satisfy the heartiest of appetites.

Your Scandinavian Dinner Menu
for 6 People at 7 P.M.

CUCUMBER SALAD WITH PICKLED BEETS
HERRING & CRACKERS · SWEDISH MEATBALLS
SCANDINAVIAN BROWN BEANS
SWEDISH RYE BREAD & BUTTER
DANISH CREAM · SERVE WITH MILK TO DRINK

(Remove berries from freezer at 5:00.)

DAY BEFORE

DANISH CREAM

HAVE READY		YOU'LL NEED
1 cup whipping cream, unwhipped	½ teaspoon vanilla	medium saucepan with lid
1 cup sugar	2 10-ounce packages of sweetened frozen	measuring cups
1 envelope unflavored gelatin	raspberries or strawberries,	large mixing spoon measuring spoons
1 cup dairy sour cream	defrosted	6 small bowls

Combine the unwhipped whipping cream with the sugar and gelatin in the saucepan. Heat over medium heat, stirring constantly until all the gelatin and sugar dissolve. Do not let it boil. Remove the pan from the heat and cool for 15 minutes. Add the sour cream and vanilla. Stir until well blended. Cover and put in the refrigerator until you are ready to serve. Spoon the cream into 6 small bowls. Top with the defrosted berries and juice.

CUCUMBER SALAD WITH PICKLED BEETS

HAVE READY

2 cucumbers
1 cup white vinegar
½ cup sugar
1 teaspoon salt
½ teaspoon pepper
2 teaspoons dried dill weed
lettuce, washed and dried
  on paper towels
1 16-ounce can sliced pickled beets

YOU'LL NEED

vegetable peeler 6 dinner
paring knife   plates
medium bowl
measuring cups
measuring spoons
small bowl
mixing spoon
paper towels
can opener

Peel cucumbers and slice into thin rounds. Be very careful. Put into medium bowl. Mix vinegar, sugar, salt, pepper and dill weed in small bowl. Pour mixture over sliced cucumbers. Put in the refrigerator for at least 3 hours. To serve, place a washed and dried lettuce leaf on each dinner plate. Top each lettuce leaf with some of the marinated cucumbers. Arrange several slices of pickled beets around the cucumbers. Set plates at the table.

SWEDISH MEATBALLS

HAVE READY

1 egg
4 tablespoons chopped onion
1 cup mashed potatoes (Follow
  the recipe for 2 persons on box
  of instant mashed potatoes, or
  use leftover mashed potatoes.)
3 tablespoons fine, dried
  bread crumbs

1 pound extra lean
  ground beef
⅓ cup whipping cream,
  unwhipped
1 teaspoon salt
fresh parsley

YOU'LL NEED

large mixing bowl 2 pot holders
fork   spatula
paring knife   serving platter
chopping board
measuring spoons
measuring cups
mixing spoon
flat pan

Break the egg into a large mixing bowl and beat lightly with a fork. Add all the other ingredients. Mix well. You can do this with your hands, **but** be sure they are clean. Next, take a small amount of the mixture in your hands and shape into meatballs about the size of a walnut. Place the meatballs in the bottom of a flat pan. Set aside. At 6:20, preheat the oven to 400°. At 6:30, bake the meatballs for 20 minutes or until browned. Remove the pan from the oven and with a spatula, put the meatballs on a serving platter and decorate with parsley.

JUST BETWEEN US: For something a little special, try combining 1 can of cream of mushroom soup with 1 cup of dairy sour cream. Heat over medium-low heat until hot. Makes a great gravy for your meatballs.

HERRING & CRACKERS

HAVE READY

2 6-ounce jars of
pickled herring
crackers

YOU'LL NEED

paring knife   small fork for
bowl for herring   herring
plate for crackers   6 small napkins

Cut herring into bite-size pieces. Put in small bowl.
Place crackers on a plate. To serve, pass herring and
crackers to your guests before they go to the table.

SCANDINAVIAN BROWN BEANS

YOU'LL NEED

small skillet
paper towel
can opener
medium saucepan
measuring cups
measuring spoons
mixing spoon
serving dish

HAVE READY

¼ cup diced, crisp fried
bacon (about 4 slices)
2 1-pound cans of red
kidney beans
¾ cup firmly packed
brown sugar
¼ teaspoon ground
cinnamon
¼ teaspoon ground
nutmeg
3 tablespoons cider
vinegar
¼ teaspoon salt
¼ teaspoon pepper

Fry bacon and drain on paper towel. Open
beans and pour off most of the juice. Then
put beans and the remaining juice into the
saucepan. Add all the other ingredients. Mix
well. Cook, uncovered, over medium heat for
30 minutes. Stir often. Pour into serving
dish.

OLD BELIEF:
To stop a quarrel,
throw some salt
in the fire.

SWEDISH RYE BREAD & BUTTER

HAVE READY

1 loaf of Swedish Rye
or Plain Rye Bread,
sliced
butter or margarine

YOU'LL NEED

bread basket
butter dish
butter knife

At dinner time, arrange
the bread in a bread bas-
ket and put butter on the
butter dish along with a
knife. Place on the table.

AMERICA

The United States is a very young country which has been termed the "melting pot" of the world. This definition could well be used to describe American cookery, too. With the immigrants who arrived from Europe, the Orient and South America have come the inspiration for many, many dishes. Once settled in a new land, these people were faced with substituting the ingredients in their family recipes with whatever was available in the new country, thereby creating new "American" dishes. In fact, very few native dishes have survived in their pure form once they became nationally popular.

Fried chicken, long considered as "American as apple pie," did not in fact originate here. It closely resembles a Viennese dish, "Wiener Backhendl," which has been a favorite in Austria for generations. We have made it our own dish, however, and it has become a part of our tradition.

American cooking was essentially simple in its beginnings when pioneers were faced with surviving the natural hardships of an untamed country. Since those times, a brief 200 years ago, we have progressed to a lifestyle filled with goodness and bounty. As a young cook in a rich and plentiful country, you are part of a delicious, continuing tradition which has only just begun.

Your U.S.A. Menu
for 4 People at 7 P.M.

OVEN-FRIED CHICKEN
CANDIED YAMS · GREEN BEANS
APPLE CRISP
SERVED WITH MILK TO DRINK

APPLE CRISP

HAVE READY

¾ cup all-purpose flour
1 cup sugar
½ teaspoon ground
  cinnamon
½ teaspoon ground nutmeg
¼ teaspoon salt
⅓ cup butter or margarine,
  melted
6 cups peeled, cored and
  sliced red apples (Wine-
  sap or Rome Beauty)

YOU'LL NEED

1½-quart oven casserole
measuring cups
measuring spoons
mixing bowl
mixing spoon
small saucepan
fork
vegetable peeler
paring knife
2 pot holders
4 serving plates

Set the oven at 400°. Grease the inside of the casserole with butter or margarine and set aside. Mix the flour, sugar, cinnamon, nutmeg and salt together in mixing bowl. Pour the melted butter or margarine over this and mix lightly with a fork. Set aside. Peel and quarter the apples. Remove the core from each quarter. Slice each quarter into 3 or 4 pieces. Place the slices of apple in the casserole. Sprinkle the flour mixture over the apples as evenly as possible. Put the casserole in the oven and bake for 35 minutes or until the apples are tender and the topping browned. (To test apples, prick with a fork. If they feel soft, they are done.) Do not refrigerate before serving. Serve warm or at room temperature.

OVEN-FRIED CHICKEN

YOU'LL NEED

small saucepan
measuring cups
measuring spoons
paper bag
pastry brush
plate
large shallow
  baking pan
2 pot holders
tongs
serving platter

HAVE READY

¼ cup butter or
  margarine, melted
1 teaspoon salt
¼ teaspoon pepper
1 cup crushed
  cornflakes
1 2½- to 3-pound
  broiler-fryer
  chicken, cut up

Melt butter or margarine in the small saucepan. Add salt and pepper. Place crushed cornflakes in a clean, strong paper bag. Brush chicken with the butter mixture using a pastry brush. Shake 3 or 4 pieces of chicken at a time in the bag to coat thoroughly, then put on a plate. Continue doing this until all the pieces of chicken are coated. Place chicken pieces skin-side-up in the ungreased, large shallow baking pan so that they do not touch each other. Bake at 375° for 1 hour. Do not turn. Remove chicken with tongs to the serving platter.

*Round as a saucer,
deep as a cup,
All the Mississippi
River
can't fill it up.*

A SIEVE

CANDIED YAMS

HAVE READY
⅓ cup butter or
  margarine
⅓ cup firmly packed
  brown sugar
½ teaspoon salt
1 1-pound, 7-ounce
  can yams or sweet
  potatoes

YOU'LL NEED
9-inch skillet
measuring cups
measuring spoons
mixing spoon
can opener
spatula
serving dish

Melt the butter or margarine in the skillet over medium heat. Add the brown sugar and salt and stir. Add the yams or sweet potatoes, placing them in one layer in the sauce. Heat through, then carefully turn the yams with a spatula. Continue cooking for about 10 minutes, until hot and bubbly and the syrup thickens. Remove to a serving dish and serve.

On the hill sits a green house,
In the green house sits a white house,
In the white house sits a red house,
In the red house are a lot of little
black and white men.

A WATERMELON

GREEN BEANS

HAVE READY
1 10-ounce package frozen
  French-style green beans
Salt and butter to taste

YOU'LL NEED
saucepan with lid
serving dish

Cook beans according to package directions. Add salt and butter to taste.

JUST BETWEEN US: Fry 3 or 4 slices of bacon until crisp, drain on paper towel and crumble over hot beans.

22

Glossary

APPETIZER: An "appetizer" is a food or drink served before the meal.

BAKE: When the recipe says to "bake" a dish, that means to cook it in the oven. Check your recipe to see what the correct temperature should be and then set your oven at **exactly** that temperature. The word "roast" is often used to mean baking meat in the oven.

BEAT: To "beat" a mixture, you should use a spoon, fork or electric mixer and stir it hard.

BLEND: When you "blend" a mixture, you don't need to stir it as hard as when you "beat," but you do stir it until all the ingredients are mixed together and there are no lumps.

BOIL: To "boil" a liquid, heat it until it begins to bubble and is very hot. Be careful.

BROWN: Several recipes will say "brown." This means cook the food until it is a nice brown color. Watch it closely so it doesn't burn.

CASSEROLE: A "casserole" is a dish with a lid that you can cook in and then serve in. The word "casserole" also refers to the food cooked. A "casserole" is usually a mixture of food.

CHILL: To "chill" a food, refrigerate it until it is cold but not frozen.

CHOP: To "chop" something, take a small, sharp knife and cut it into small pieces. Whenever chopping, use a wooden chopping board and be very careful. The word "dice" means to chop into **very** small pieces.

COLANDER: A colander is a large strainer. You can use a colander to drain anything you have cooked in water. Set the colander in the sink and pour what you want to drain right into the colander. You can also use the colander to keep cooked food warm by placing the food in the colander and setting it in a saucepan with warm water in the bottom over low heat on the stove.

COMBINE: To "combine" ingredients, use a spoon and mix them all together.

DISSOLVE: When you "dissolve" an ingredient, you let it melt in a liquid.

DOUBLE BOILER: A double boiler is two saucepans which fit together, one on top of the other. You should put about two inches of water in the bottom saucepan, and the ingredients you are cooking in the top saucepan. Heat the water until it is hot enough to cook what is in the top half. The purpose of a double boiler is to be able to cook something so that it won't stick or cook too fast.

DUST: This means to sprinkle very lightly. To "dust" with powdered sugar means to sprinkle the sugar all over the item.

ENTRÉE: After you serve an appetizer and salad or soup, you are ready to serve the "entrée." This is the main part of the meal.

FOLD IN: Sometimes the recipe will say "fold in" the whipped cream or some other ingredient. To do this, take a mixing spoon and with a circular motion very gently stir the ingredient into the mixture.

FRY: To "fry" means to cook food in hot oil or shortening in a skillet.